Old NEWPORT and WORMI[T]

by
Mairi Shiels

The pierhead, Newport.

© Mairi Shiels 1998
First published in the United Kingdom, 1998,
by Stenlake Publishing, Ochiltree Sawmill, The Lade,
Ochiltree, Ayrshire, KA18 2NX
Telephone / Fax: 01290 423114

ISBN 1 84033 049 X

ACKNOWLEDGEMENTS

The author would like to thank William Owen for his advice.

The publishers would like to thank Ian Lindsay, whose collection of postcards of Newport and Wormit form the majority of those reproduced in this book.

THE PUBLISHERS REGRET THAT THEY CANNOT SUPPLY COPIES OF ANY PICTURES FEATURED IN THIS BOOK.

A more impressive sight than the trickle it has become today, this burn once turned the water wheel which powered the corn mills that stood in the pier area - hence Newport's earlier name of Seamills. Latterly the wheel powered the tools of the smiddy. The wheel and smiddy both belonged to the Tayfield Estate but passed into the ownership of the town council. The smiddy stopped working in the 1940s and the water wheel was dismantled in the 1950s.

INTRODUCTION

Most of the development of Newport and Wormit has occurred during the last two hundred years. Prior to 1800, there were settlements at both Seamills, the earlier name for the area around the pier at Newport, and at Woodhaven. Both of these communities centred on the ferry services they provided to Dundee, and on the salmon fishing which took place all along the coast.

There had been some attempt at development of Seamills in the seventeenth and eighteenth centuries, when the Dundee magistrates leased the corn mills there. To cope with the increased traffic across the river at that time, the Dundee Guildry built a new pier and inn and hoped to develop the area commercially, thus opening up a new market for Dundee traders. The venture proved a failure, but, in addition to the pier and inn, one legacy of the scheme was the change of name, first from Seamills to New Dundee, then to Newport-Dundee and finally to Newport.

At the beginning of the nineteenth century there were probably only about twenty or thirty cottages scattered around Newport and Woodhaven. Situated on the hill overlooking Newport pier was Tayfield House, newly built in 1788 by John Berry. Most of the population would have been boatmen or fishermen, and some were tradesmen. Many would have been involved in spinning and weaving, and agriculture and whinstone quarrying would have provided some employment too.

Fierce competition existed between the two rival ferry services, with Woodhaven tending to be more popular, especially after 1790 when a turnpike road was built to the harbour there. It was the building of the turnpike road to Newport in 1808 and the establishment of the more modern steam ferry service of the 1820s which confirmed Newport as the most important ferry crossing point on the river for a century and a half. The increase in ferry traffic and connecting coach traffic encouraged building, especially in East Newport, and led to the first stage of development of the village as it appears today. Newport began to establish itself as a dormitory suburb of Dundee and a convenient holiday resort for Dundee businessmen.

From the middle of the century onwards, when plans for a railway bridge were becoming a reality, the village experienced its second major period of expansion. Extensive building took place, both further along the shore to the east and west, and uphill. Many of the more elegant villas, rising from the river in terraces, were built at this time. The building of the bridge, and of the station at Wormit, also encouraged the development of Wormit.

In 1887 Newport acquired the status of a police burgh, and for much of the twentieth century, until local government reorganisation of 1975, the affairs of the village were managed first of all by the police commissioners and then by the elected town council. In 1902 the burgh boundaries were extended to include Woodhaven and Wormit. During its years in operation the council energetically addressed a huge range of issues including problems concerning housing, traffic management, street maintenance and provision of leisure facilities.

Since the Second World War, one of the more obvious changes in the area has been the extensive - some would say excessive - building of both council and private housing. The two communities, which were once separated by green fields, are now joined by continuous housing. Another major change was the opening of the Tay Road Bridge in August 1966. The new bridge made the ferries, and eventually the railway too, redundant. Newport and Wormit are now more easily accessible to travellers, and are as much convenient places of residence for Dundee businesspeople as they ever were. The villages have certainly experienced changes in the last thirty years, but these have probably got as much to do with general progress as the building of the road bridge.

Wormit Farm

The approach to Wormit along an almost unrecognisably peaceful Kilmany Road. Wormit Farm on the left is still there, but the appearance of both sides of the road has been altered by the ribbon development of 1920s bungalows. Until the building of the new approach road from Sandford to the Tay Road Bridge in the 1960s, this was the main road into the villages from the south.

Wormit and Golf Course from North

Like many other open spaces in the district, Wormit Golf Course was a casualty of World War Two's 'Dig for Victory' campaign, when people were encouraged to plough up any available land for food production. The club was in existence from 1912 until 1939, and could boast in its information for members that it was the nearest golf course to Dundee City Centre, the first tee being only fifteen minutes away by train.

JV 1863

Opened in June 1878, and hailed as a wonder of the age, the first Tay Railway Bridge was in use for just eighteen months. The disastrous storm of Sunday 28 December 1879 threw the central thirteen spans into the river, taking a train from Burntisland and seventy-five men, women and children with it. During construction of the bridge it was discovered that, contrary to pre-building surveys, there was not a bed of rock stretching all the way across the river. There was therefore no sound base on which to position the heavy brick pillars, so it was decided to change the design and use iron columns, which would exert less pressure, for the central section of the bridge. This decision was later proved to be a contributory factor in its collapse. The two types of pillars can be seen in this photograph.

Tay Bridge Disaster. 1879.

The central section of the bridge fell into the river almost intact, with most of the ill-fated train still enclosed within the tunnel-like high girders. The section shown here was photographed on Broughty Ferry beach. An accurate count of the lives lost was made by adding up the tickets collected from Dundee-bound passengers at St Fort station, the train's last stop before the bridge. The first body was washed up on the shore at Newport the next day, but it was weeks before others were found, and in all only forty-six bodies were ever recovered. During the days following the disaster a huge collection of clothing and personal effects, including a Bible, spectacles, keys, luggage and a hand muff containing a love letter, was washed up on Broughty Ferry beach. The pipe on the right carried the water supply to Newport.

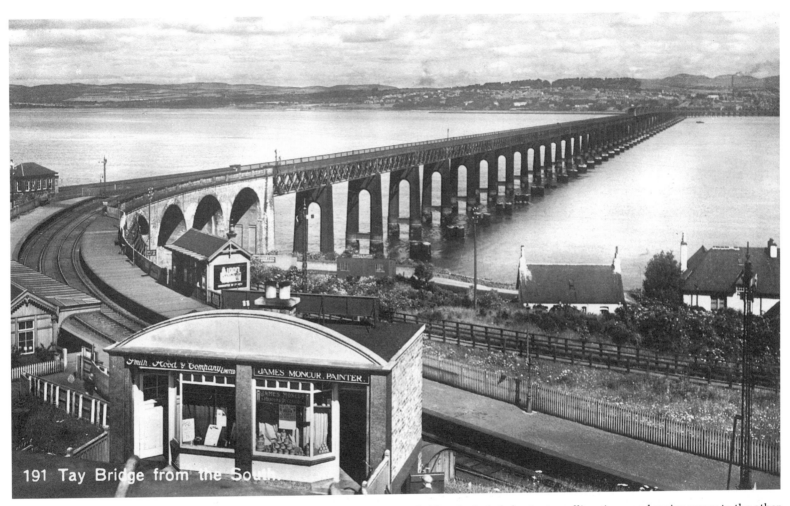

191 Tay Bridge from the South.

During its short lifetime, the benefits of the bridge had been much appreciated. They included shorter travelling times and easier access to the other side of the river for the people of Fife and Dundee, the fresh water supply which was carried over the bridge to Newport and Wormit, and a ready means of supplying coal to Dundee industrialists. It was very soon decided therefore to replace the bridge. The new bridge, which opened in June 1887, was of a more solid construction. The foundations and piers were much stronger and stringent safety inspections were carried out at every stage of the building work.

This picture, taken from the station, shows the sharpness of the curve which trains had to negotiate after leaving Wormit Station before entering the tunnel *en route* to West Newport, the next stop on the line. Over the years the tunnel and curve were the scene of several accidents. Perhaps the most serious occurred in May 1955 when 500 children and helpers from three Dundee Sunday schools were returning from their annual picnic at Tayport. The train crashed as it emerged from the tunnel. Two men and a boy were killed, and many were injured.

CROSSHILL TERRACE, WORMIT.

Most of Crosshill Terrace dates from the early 1900s. The house nearest the camera was used for some time as the manse, but the manses in Wormit seem to have moved with the ministers. On the right is the unexpectedly named Reservoir Road. When the first railway bridge was built it was decided to pipe water across the bridge from Dundee to serve the needs of the growing communities of Newport and Wormit. Accordingly a pipe was laid over the bridge and a reservoir built up on Wormit Hill in the 1870s by the Dundee Water Commissioners. One of Wormit's claims to fame is that it was the first village in Scotland to have electricity. This was provided by Alexander Stewart, owner of the Tayside Electric Company, and a Dundee builder who built many of the turn of the century Wormit houses. His electricity-powered houses are still easily spotted in Wormit today - his trademark was the rising sun pattern on the woodwork above upstairs windows. The best examples are in Hillpark Terrace.

Newport Road, Wormit.

75604. J.V.

Although the cottages on the left of this picture still look remarkably similar, there has been much change in the field opposite over the last century. As the village population increased at the end of the nineteenth century a new school was required. This site was chosen and Wormit Public School opened here in 1896, a spacious improvement over the school's temporary accommodation in a hut at the railway cottages and in Stewart's hall. The school served the village until 1978, by which time further population increases had led to overcrowding. A new school was built on the hill behind and the old one demolished.

At Woodhaven, Newport, Fife

A peaceful spot on the wooded shore west of Woodhaven pier. Until 1820 there was a regular ferry service to Dundee from Woodhaven, and in fact until the early 1800s the Woodhaven service tended to be more popular than the one from Newport. This was emphasised in 1790 when a good turnpike road was built over Flass Hill into Woodhaven, thus connecting it with other roads south and giving it a distinct advantage over Newport. The toll-house for this road was situated at the top of the hill leading down to the pier. The area around Woodhaven pier is now used mainly by Wormit Boating Club. During the Second World War Norwegian forces were stationed at Woodhaven. They serviced the Catalina flying boats of the No. 333 Norwegian Squadron as they returned from their sorties over the North Sea and secret missions into enemy-occupied Norway. A close link was forged between the Norwegians and local people which is still maintained today.

The Training Ship *Mars* was moored out in the river off Woodhaven pier from 1869 until 1929, and provided a home for anything up to 400 'at-risk' boys at a time. Contrary to popular belief, the boys were not all juvenile delinquents, but perhaps came from broken homes or had a history of school truanting. The regime was strict and the discipline hard, and no doubt these local boys 'skinny-dipping' off the end of the pier were thankful they were not subject to it.

Woodhaven, Wormit.

The *Mars* boys received a naval training, and always provided teams to compete in local regattas. On the shore here, and conveniently close to the pier, is the building that originally served as the St Fort Estate granary, but which was used from 1883 onwards as a hospital for the *Mars* boys. Prior to the establishment of the hospital, it had proved extremely difficult to contain any outbreaks of infectious diseases on board ship. The granary had previously been used as hostel accommodation for the men building the railway bridge.

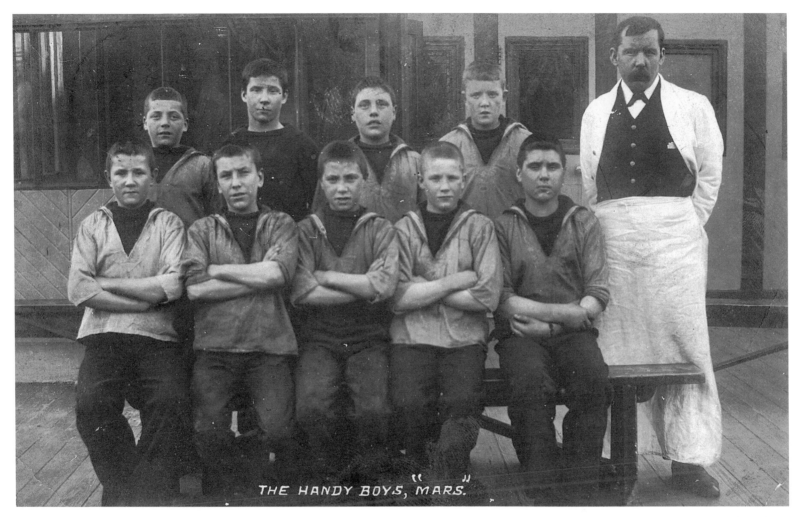

THE HANDY BOYS, "MARS."

As well as naval skills, the boys received training in woodwork, metalwork, shoe-making and tailoring. Extensive workshops were constructed on-shore at Woodhaven and items made by the *Mars* boys can still be found in local households. Here they are seen with one of their instructors. Garden ground was cultivated at Woodhaven where they produced vegetables for their own use and for sale - hence the present day street name 'Mars Gardens'. While on board they were known only by a number, wore a naval-type uniform and sported uniform haircuts. This postcard view was sent all the way to Calcutta.

Mars Training Ship. DUNDEE. A.M.A.

This unusual picture has the *Mars* boys spelling out a seasonal message. Carefully arranged on the railway embankment above Woodhaven, they were also photographed in a 'Happy Christmas' pose. During their annual summer camp at the granary at Elie, the boys repeated this performance, but instead they spelled out 'Best Wishes' to the people of Elie.

The first house on the right on entering Newport is Hollybank, fairly recently built when this early 1900s photograph was taken. It became the home of Dr Montague Rust. He was fairly unconventional for his day (and for Newport) as he was a great believer in, and practitioner of, spiritualism and faith healing. It is said that he had a neon sign in his garden advertising his services. Beyond Hollybank is The Castle, probably dating from 1812, and named simply for its appearance rather than any function as a fortified building.

Much of the housing in this part of West Newport was built and owned by the Just family. The first two blocks here, as well as the terrace beyond, were all built by members of that family. In the late 1950s Just's Land, on the right, and River House, centre, were declared unfit for habitation and demolished. Plans to rebuild on the land were abandoned when it was decided that the site was unsuitable.

Balmore is the most westerly of the three large mansion houses at the end of West Road. It was built in the 1870s for William Robertson, an iron-founder and ex-provost of Dundee, and is the only one of the three still used as a private house. Although this photograph was taken at the entrance to Balmore, it is not known whether the passengers are connected with the Robertson family.

Kinbrae Newport, Fife.

Kinbrae was built for Sir John Leng, editor and general manager of the *Dundee Advertiser* and also founder of the *Evening Telegraph* and *People's Friend*. Between 1889 and 1906 he was Liberal MP in Dundee, eventually losing his seat to Winston Churchill. The grounds at Kinbrae were often used for fetes and garden parties, particularly in connection with the local Liberal Association. Despite various suggestions in the 1950s for alternative uses for the building - among them a remand home, a hotel and overspill accommodation for the school - the house was demolished in 1960 and is now the site of Kinbrae Park housing estate.

WESTWOOD, NEWPORT, FIFE.

Now more familiarly known as St Serf's Home, Westwood was built for Harry Walker, a jute manufacturer in Dundee. The wealthiest of the jute barons tended to head for Broughty Ferry and build their mansions there, but there is no doubt that Newport, with its clean air, provided an attractive alternative to the smokier north shore of the Tay. St Serf's has been a residential home for the elderly since the 1940s.

THE PIER, NEWPORT.

Ferries had already been crossing the Tay at this point for hundreds of years when a more modern, efficient service from Newport was established in the 1820s. The introduction of the first steamship on the crossing, the *Union*, confirmed Newport's place as the most important crossing point on the river, and finally ended the old rivalry with Woodhaven. The ferries served the village until the opening of the Tay Road Bridge in 1966, and are remembered with much nostalgia.

The Pier, Newport

The new ferry service of the 1820s led to a need for improved facilities at Newport, and in 1823 work started on the construction of a pier designed by Thomas Telford. Looking down upon the pier are Seamills Cottages and, further away, the tower of Westwood. Berthed here is the *Dundee*, which served on the crossing from 1875 until 1917. She had the distinction of being the first ship on the scene of the disaster when the rail bridge fell. During almost 150 years thirteen boats were in operation, but it was the seventy year service of the *Fifeshire* which earned the ferry to Dundee the affectionate name of the Fifie. All were paddle steamers, apart from the last two, the diesel-powered *Abercraig* and *Scotscraig*, both of which were much larger and designed to carry more motor vehicles.

Dundee Fire Brigade at Newport Pier

The ferries provided a vital link between Fife and Angus, and on occasions the Dundee Fire Brigade turned out to deal with fires in Newport or Wormit. Their arrival was clearly an event of interest to onlookers.

A circus on the move was a not unusual sight in the earlier years of this century, with the animals travelling on foot from town to town. It was quite common for children to be allowed out of school to see them pass, but there would appear to be plenty opportunity to view them here as they wait patiently for the Fifie. The camel has apparently experienced all the attention before. The chemist shop at the pier was conveniently placed for passing trade, but on one occasion it was just too convenient; the Fifie rammed into the back of it and caused considerable damage. The ornate pier buildings were built in the 1870s, and the area around them soon became the centre of village life. As well as the chemist the pier buildings and those opposite housed a butcher, baker, fishmonger, painter, optician, and the post office and police station.

EAST NEWPORT, FIFE

How well dressed are these sailors of almost a century ago! On the left of the picture is the old granary. The chimney belonged to the gasworks, which supplied the village with gas from the 1850s onwards. The works later moved to a new site on the Tayport road. All the buildings in this area to the rear of the Newport Inn were demolished, and the land used for the Granary Lane housing development.

The old post office here was run for many years by 'Postie Anderson'. He was a keen photographer and was responsible for many of the old photographs and postcard views of the village which survive today. There is still a reminder of the post office in the old stamp machines which remain on the wall. Beyond the post office is the mission hall, and, tucked in out of sight, the smiddy. John T. Young's cycle repair shop is just visible. The enterprising Mr Young subsequently concentrated on developing his motor repair business. He was a well-respected figure in the community, serving on the town council from 1918 until 1941 (including three years as provost), as well as on many committees including those of the curling club, Liberal Association and, of course, the cycling club.

The granary and gasworks were situated conveniently close to the old pier, built by the Dundee magistrates in the early 1700s when they leased the corn mills nearby. Following the construction of Telford's pier in the 1820s, the old pier continued to be used for commercial purposes until World War One, after which it fell into disrepair. Now only a few stumps can be seen at low tide.

The Tayfield Estate was formed in 1788 when John Berry bought the land of Inverdovat and built his house, naming it Tayfield. The original estate was extensive, covering most of Newport as we know it today, plus land stretching beyond Inverdovat, Causewayhead and Chesterhill. The grounds around the house were developed throughout the nineteenth century, with some areas being landscaped and a particularly impressive programme of tree-planting implemented. The north and south lodges date from 1821 and 1830. Gradually the estate decreased in size, with land being feued or sold for house-building, and gifted or leased for leisure use.

Between 1828 and 1830 extensive alterations were made to Tayfield House. The roof was modified, the west side extended and a completely new south front added. On the left of this picture is the large Victorian summer-house. The church-like windows are exactly what they seem! When the new Forgan church opened in 1841 the contents of the old kirk on the back road to Tayport were auctioned off. Even the windows were sold and, as can be seen here, they were put to good use. There are other reminders of days past elsewhere in the grounds - the remains of the two curling ponds used by the local curling club, the delightful multi-coloured bee-house and an ice-house, later used for storing coal!

Between 1868 and 1893 Newport experienced a tremendous flurry of church-building, with six churches being built in just twenty-five years. On the left here is St Mary's Episcopal Church, opened in 1887. Behind St Mary's manse is the Congregational Church at the foot of Kilnburn, built in 1868, closed in 1986 and demolished in 1991. Just making an appearance on the right is the entrance to Trinity Church, built in 1881. The church was preceded by Newport's first post office and, prior to that, by an earlier Newport Inn. The small building opposite, which accommodated a wide variety of shops and services over the years, was originally the Tayfield Estate office.

HIGH STREET, NEWPORT.

88606. JK

Judging by the style of dress, this picture of the High Street probably dates from the 1920s. At the bottom of the street on the right is the Newport Inn, which bears the date 1806, although sadly now barely legible. It was originally a coaching inn, built by the first Mr Berry to take advantage of the gradually increasing coach and ferry traffic. Although a particularly attractive feature of the High Street, the trees became increasingly impractical as traffic increased, and were finally removed in the late 1960s to allow road widening. Perhaps the recent arrival of the boat would account for the huge numbers of pedestrians flocking up the street. They may well be day-trippers enjoying an outing on the Fifie.

As Newport's population grew through the nineteenth century, the parish church at Forgan could not meet its needs, so a new church, St Thomas's, was built in the village. At first St Thomas's did not have a manse, but in 1901 a Grand Bazaar raised enough money to build one, extend the church and install an organ! Rev. Thomas Fraser was the church's first minister and gave faithful service for forty-two years until he died in 1913. St Thomas's, having united with the Forgan church and St Fillan's (Free) church, is now Newport Parish Church.

FORGAN NEAR NEWPORT.

Forgan Parish School, above, was the main school in the parish until 1843 when St Fillan's Free Church was built in William Street. St Fillan's established a school in their church hall which gradually came to cater for the village children, while Forgan attracted the country children. Both schools were supervised by their ministers and kirk sessions. The children here look well turned out but keeping the girls' white pinafores clean must have been difficult. It was common custom to wear them right-side-out on Monday and Tuesday, inside-out on Wednesday and Thursday, and whichever way was cleaner on Friday!

The Education Act of 1842 legislated for school boards to be established to oversee education in every parish. Following this the school board took over responsibility for the William Street and Forgan schools, and in 1879 opened this fine new school in Blyth Street. It replaced the William Street school which was then used for congregational purposes. Until 1949 Newport Higher Grade School provided a full education, covering all subjects, until third year in secondary, after which pupils travelled to Dundee, Cupar or St Andrews. This school closed in 1977 when the new primary school was built. Just beyond the school is the Blyth Hall, gifted to the people of Newport in 1877 by Mrs Blyth-Martin, and seen here without its 1970s front extension.

This view was probably taken from the tower of St Thomas's church. Much of the area east of Cupar Road was planned and developed in the 1820s and 1830s. It was named Maryton after the landowner's wife, and three streets were called after his sons William, Robert and James. Most prominent in the picture is St Fillan's Free Church, standing at the junction of King Street and William Street, and established in 1843 after the Disruption which split the Church of Scotland. This church was erected in 1868 and replaced an earlier temporary structure. Next door (just visible between the two villas on the left of the picture) is the hall where the Free Church school operated for so many years, now converted to housing. The church was demolished in 1979.

St.Phillan's Place, Newport-on-Tay.

693/25

A fascinating pre-First World War picture, with a horse-drawn delivery cart on the right. Wallace's shoe shop operated from 1900 until the 1960s. On the left is Robertson Place, a row of shops built around 1900 and named after Alexander Robertson the builder. Until the 1920s the upper storey housed the Unionist Party's club-rooms, after which the property was sold to St Thomas's church, renamed Kirk House, and used as much needed hall accommodation. In 1992 it was converted to housing. Until the 1890s a toll-house stood on this site, and prior to that the toll-bar here had stopped travellers on the turnpike road down to Newport pier. The railings around St Thomas's church, like many others in the village, were removed for World War Two's metal salvage collection. Whether they ever formed part of a Spitfire remains a mystery!

Newport Bowling Club was founded in 1869 and the bowling green opened in 1877; the club had 100 members by 1890. Money for the green was raised by the sale of £1 shares. There had been an earlier bowling club in East Newport in the grounds of Seacraig House, a substantial mansion which stood between Union Street and King Street, now the site of Seacraig Court. This photograph probably dates from the 1890s or 1900. The house immediately behind on Cupar Road was originally called Woodbank, although it was named Hillpark when this photograph was taken, and was latterly called Rolleston. During World War Two it was used as a hostel for evacuees.

A very early view of East Newport station. The first houses in Norwood were built in the early 1890s so this picture certainly pre-dates that. The line from the Tay Bridge through Newport to Tayport was built in 1879, and the first station-master here was James Duncan. He earned £50 a year and was also provided with a house. The railway company allowed their agents to trade in coal - hence the Coal Depot sign. Mr Duncan was one of the first to see the fallen railway bridge. On the evening of the disaster a friend reported seeing the bridge fall, and the two men walked along the line to Wormit to witness the scale of the disaster for themselves.

In the early days there was only a single platform at East Newport, staffed by Mr Duncan and two assistants. As the village expanded, so too did the facilities at the station, as can be seen in this 1906 picture. The railway certainly helped in the development of the village, as James Duncan recalled: 'For the first few years, trainload after trainload of bricks, stones and other building materials arrived every week'. The line to Newport closed in 1969, surviving only three years after the opening of the road bridge. The continuation to Tayport had closed in 1966 to allow the construction of the bridge access road.

RAILWAY STATION WEST NEWPORT, FIFE.

West Newport station was situated at the top of Kinbrae Park, and the eagle-eyed can still spot the concrete West Newport sign lying in the grass at the side of the nature trail. The vessel on the river is the *Vulcan*, the repairs ship for pre-First World War submarines based on the Tay. The elevated position of the railway line through Newport provided magnificent views over the river. A combined season ticket for rail and ferry travel was available, so the less energetically inclined Dundee commuters could walk downhill to catch the ferry to Dundee, travel back by train and walk downhill to reach home.

THE BRAES, NEWPORT

B. 1821

The deserted Braes of 1990s summer afternoons make it difficult to appreciate how popular the area was for picnics earlier this century - popular not only with locals but with visitors too. A favourite excursion for Dundonians was a trip on the Fifie and a picnic at Newport, usually on the Braes but often in Windmill Park, the village park beyond the present-day dual carriageway. Local confectioners took advantage of the crowds and set up stalls and barrows on Tay Street to sell ice-cream and sweets. The Braes originally belonged to Tayfield Estate but were given to the village in 1946. On the right of the picture is the war memorial, designed by Robert Lorimer and unveiled in 1922.

The busiest days on the Braes were on the occasions of the annual regattas and swimming galas. Spectators chose the best vantage points, sometimes clambering out on to Big Rock, the starting point for races and where they were ensured a good view. The swimming club had a diving stage and two changing huts, and one of Newport's attractions to its nineteenth century settlers was the fine sea-bathing it offered. The boating club had a shed and slipway, and on regatta days crews came from miles around to compete. The club folded in the 1920s.

Bathing Station, Newport

Rather an uninviting-looking day at the bathing station. The name Royal Hotel can just be made out on the old Royal Buildings at the corner of Tay Street and Robert Street. Built in 1877, the buildings housed the Royal Hotel, Royal Café, and various shops and businesses over the years, and were sometimes called Turnbull's Buildings after the builder. When they were demolished in the 1970s, a glass carboy containing 1877 newspapers and a memorandum signed by John Turnbull was found in the foundations.

The back of this card explains that these are Dundee jute girls enjoying a day out on Newport Braes. For the jute workers especially, so used to the noise, smell and pollution of the mills, Newport, with its clean sea breezes, must have seemed like another world. These young lasses look particularly happy and innocent, but in fact the town council had to deal with frequent complaints from residents about the rowdy and often drunken behaviour of visitors. In 1914 it was decided to close local pubs on Dundee holidays in order to discourage the rowdier visitors.

St Fort House, just to the south of Newport and Wormit, was built by Henry Stewart around 1850. The Stewart family owned much of the land on which Wormit and West Newport developed. They lived in the house until about 1900, after which the Pilkington family occupied it. During World War Two the RAF made use of the house, and in the post-war years it was let as a hotel. This venture, however, enjoyed only limited success, and in the early 1950s the roof was removed in order to save money on rates. This led to the building's rapid deterioration and it was eventually demolished.

St Fort Creamery, Newport Fife

The approach road to the Tay Road Bridge cut through the land of the St Fort Estate. The parkland in front of the house, where the carriage-driving championships are now held, was known as 'the greens'. Looking from the main road today, the creamery is just visible. For a humble dairy, it is a most unusual little building with thatched roof supported by wooden props. The verandah was beautifully tiled and the windows were of leaded glass. Inside everything was kept spotlessly clean. The creamery supplied milk, butter and cream to the family in St Fort House and to all the other families on the estate. It was probably in use until the 1940s.

This picture brings us almost back to where we started from; heading north from here would lead back into Wormit on Kilmany Road. The present Five Roads roundabout has none of the charm of this lovely spot. With the construction of the new approach road to the Tay Road Bridge in the 1960s the area changed almost beyond recognition. Prior to that, a walk or cycle to Five Roads was a favourite Sunday excursion for Newport and Wormit residents.